WORLD CULTURES

MAORI

LESLIE STRUDWICK

www.av2books.com

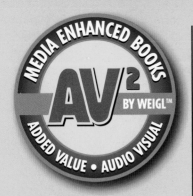

AV² provides enriched content that supplements and complements this book. Weigl's AV² books strive to create inspired learning and engage young minds in a total learning experience.

Your AV² Media Enhanced books come alive with...

Audio
Listen to sections of the book read aloud.

Key Words
Study vocabulary, and complete a matching word activity.

Video
Watch informative video clips.

Quizzes
Test your knowledge.

Embedded Weblinks
Gain additional information for research.

Slide Show
View images and captions, and prepare a presentation.

Try This!
Complete activities and hands-on experiments.

... and much, much more!

Go to www.av2books.com, and enter this book's unique code.

BOOK CODE

E 1 2 4 8 4 6

AV² by Weigl brings you media enhanced books that support active learning.

Published by AV² by Weigl
350 5th Avenue, 59th Floor
New York, NY 10118 USA
Website: www.weigl.com   www.av2books.com

Library of Congress Cataloging-in-Publication Data

Strudwick, Leslie, 1970-
 Maori / Leslie Strudwick.
    p. cm. -- (World cultures)
Includes index.
ISBN 978-1-61913-095-1 (hard cover : alk. paper) -- ISBN 978-1-61913-532-1 (soft cover : alk. paper)
1. Maori (New Zealand people) -- Juvenile literature. I. Title.
DU423.A1S77 2012
305.89'9442--dc23
                                2011051107

Printed in the United States of America in North Mankato, Minnesota
1 2 3 4 5 6 7 8 9 0   16 15 14 13 12

062012
WEP170512

Senior Editor: Heather Kissock
Art Director: Terry Paulhus

Consultant James Heremaia

Photo Credits
Weigl acknowledges Getty Images as primary photo suppliers for this title.

CONTENTS

Where in the World?

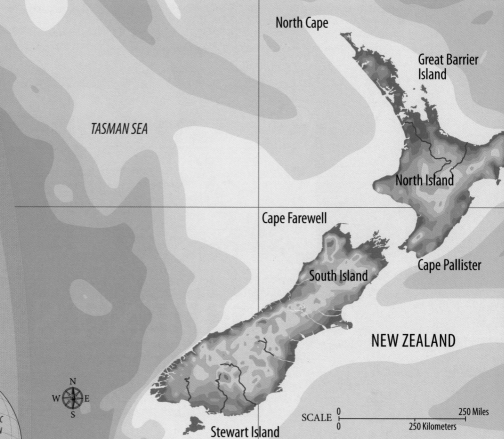

North Cape

Great Barrier Island

TASMAN SEA

North Island

Cape Farewell

Cape Pallister

South Island

NEW ZEALAND

N
W E
S

SCALE

0 _____ 250 Miles
0 _____ 250 Kilometers

Stewart Island

ASIA

PACIFIC OCEAN

INDIAN OCEAN

AUSTRALIA

NEW ZEALAND

ANTARCTICA

Population: more than 10 million
Indigenous Population (Maori): About 673,000
Region: Oceania
Country: New Zealand
Area of Oceania: 317,700 square miles (822,843 square kilometers)

New Zealand is located in the South Pacific Ocean south of the equator. New Zealand includes two large islands and many small islands. The closest large landmass is Australia, located 1,000 miles (1,609 kilometers) to the northwest. New Zealand's **indigenous peoples** are called the Maori. Although it is not certain when the Maori first began arriving on New Zealand, or **Aotearoa**, most archaeologists believe it was between AD 950 and AD 1130. Even Maori oral history and legends suggest this is the time when they traveled to Aotearoa.

The reason why the Maori peoples went to New Zealand is a mystery. However, the story of how the Maori arrived on this new land is always the same.

A group of people called Polynesians lived on some of the islands in the Pacific Ocean. The area where they lived is called Polynesia. Polynesia consists of many islands, including Tahiti, the Cook Islands, Hawai'i, and Easter Island off the coast of South America. The Polynesians were the first group of people to set sail for the distant, unsettled land of Aotearoa. They traveled in huge canoes that carried more than 100 people each. This group of Polynesian voyagers is known as the Great Fleet. While stories tell of several hundred people who arrived on Aotearoa at the same time, some researchers today believe there were much fewer people in the group.

When the Maori arrived at Aotearoa, they found a very different land than the tropical islands from which they came. The temperature was cooler, there were different plants and trees, and there were no land mammals, just reptiles, birds, and sea life. Most early Maori settled on the northern island of Aotearoa because it was warmer, but some groups settled on South Island as well.

The Maori quickly adapted to life on Aotearoa. They learned to hunt and fish the wildlife in the region. Many of the islands' birds could not fly, including a large ostrich-like bird called the **moa**. Moas were hunted and used as food. The settlers used moa bones to make tools and ornaments. They used moa eggshells to carry water.

The settlers learned to grow crops after they hunted some of the animals, such as the moa, to **extinction**. Small settlements became large villages once the Maori settled and began farming.

The Maori name for New Zealand's South Island is *Te Wai Pounamu*, which means "the Greenstone Water."

Culture Cues

🦤 Aotearoa's land area is a total of 103,470 square miles (267,990 square kilometers).

🦤 Aotearoa is home to more than 1,500 plant species that are not found anywhere else in the world. Some of these plants are the kauri, totara, and rimu.

🦤 The largest lake in Aotearoa is Lake Taupo. This lake has an area of 234 square miles (606 sq. km).

🦤 The only native land mammals on Aotearoa are bats. Humans brought all other land mammals to the islands.

Stories and Legends

Maori legends explained the relationship between people, the land, and the sea.

Like many other **cultures**, the Maori used legends to explain the origins of their culture and the creation of land, water, and humans.

According to Maori legend, in the beginning of time nothing existed, only darkness. The sea, Earth, and gods had not been created. The Moon, the Sun, and the Heavens were created from the darkness. Soon after, the first Maori people were born from this nothingness. They were the Sky Father, named Ranginui, and the Earth Mother, named Papatuanuku. The Father and the Mother embraced as they traveled to Earth. This embrace covered the sunlight, and there was darkness again.

Ranginui and Papatuanuku had 70 male children. These children became the many gods the Maori worship. Ranginui and Papatuanuku remained embraced around their children. The children tired of living in darkness. In order to have light, Ranginui and Papatuanuku's children realized they must separate their parents.

Many of the children struggled to separate Ranginui and Papatuanuku, but it was Tane-Mahuta, the god of forests, who succeeded. He believed Ranginui should live in the sky and Papatuanuku should live on Earth.

Light shone down on the children after Ranginui and Papatuanuku were separated. However, the Sky Father was heartbroken. His tears created the oceans.

Tawairi Matea, who was the god of wind and storms, was angry with his brothers for separating his parents. He created the winds and storms in revenge. Tawairi Matea decided to join his father in the sky.

After the creation of the sky and Earth, Tane realized there was something missing on Earth. He created woman from clay and breathed life into her. This Earth-formed woman was Hine-hauone. She and Tane had a daughter named Hinetitama, who later became the goddess of the night.

According to Maori legend, an ancient navigator named Kupe discovered Aotearoa while in pursuit of a giant octopus.

THE STORY OF
How Maui Discovered Aotearoa

One day when Maui was very young, he hid in his brother's fishing boat. The brothers did not find Maui until they were too far from shore to turn back.

The brothers continued rowing out to sea. Once they were quite far from shore, Maui dropped his magic fishhook into the water. Soon, he felt a strong tug on the line. Maui called to his brothers for help.

After much hard work, the brothers pulled the North Island of Aotearoa from the water. Maui thought the gods might be angry, so he went to make peace.

While Maui was gone, the brothers fought to control the land. They pounded the island with their weapons. This made mountains and valleys.

Out of the Past

Traditional Maori families lived together in villages. Each village had several tribes, or *iwi*. Each member of the iwi was related through a common **ancestor**. Each tribe was made up of many sub-tribes, or *hapu*. About 500 people lived in one hapu.

The land on which a hapu lived and farmed was owned by all the people in the tribe. Individuals did not own land. Each village settlement may have had one or many hapu.

Often, the land on which a hapu lived was valuable. This caused fighting between some tribes. Land was symbolic of power, **prestige**, and wealth. Many tribes needed more land as their villages grew. Warfare was an important aspect of Maori life. However, fighting only occurred during times when the Maori could not grow crops or hunt. The chores involved with these activities were more important than fighting.

Settling into villages changed the Maori's traditional way of life. Another important change took place when European settlers began arriving on Aotearoa.

Timeline of the Maori

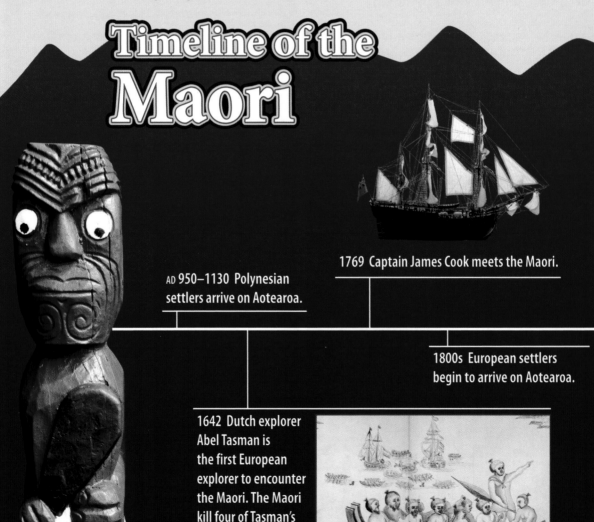

AD 950–1130 Polynesian settlers arrive on Aotearoa.

1769 Captain James Cook meets the Maori.

1800s European settlers begin to arrive on Aotearoa.

1642 Dutch explorer Abel Tasman is the first European explorer to encounter the Maori. The Maori kill four of Tasman's crew members.

In 1642, a Dutch explorer named Abel Tasman was the first European to visit the region. It was not until more than 100 years later, when Captain James Cook arrived, that the Maori felt the impact of European settlers on their culture.

The Maori called European settlers *Pakeha*. At first, the Maori welcomed the Pakeha to their land. The Europeans brought new tools and materials to the Maori. They taught the Maori new farming methods. However, the Europeans also brought diseases to the Maori. Many became ill and died after contracting these diseases.

The Europeans brought weapons and alcohol to Aotearoa. Traditionally, battles between Maori tribes were fought with spears, knives, and clubs. With the Pakehas' muskets, the Maori killed each other in record numbers during wars.

The first Christian **missionaries** arrived in New Zealand in 1814. Christian missionaries were also called Pakehas. While the Maori did not want to learn about Christianity, the missionaries taught them how to read and write. The Maori's traditional way of life was quickly disappearing.

1980s More than 90 percent of the Maori population live in cities.

1840 The Maori and the British government sign the Treaty of Waitangi, granting Great Britain rule of the island and promising the Maori British citizenship and rights.

1860–1872 The Maori fight the British in the New Zealand Wars.

1995 Queen Elizabeth II of Great Britain issues a formal apology to the Maori for their loss of lives and property in the 1800s.

1841 Aotearoa becomes a British **colony**.

1920s Maori art and culture are thriving.

1990s–2000s The government compensates the Maori with land and payments to make amends for violations of the Treaty of Waitangi.

Social Structures

Each traditional Maori village followed a specific structure. Villages were fortified to protect them from attack by other Maori tribes. These villages were called *pa*. Within the village, there was a main meeting house called a *whare*. If the village was large, there might be more than one whare. A whare was usually located in the center of a village. The Maori built a large, public meeting area, called a *marae*, in front of the whare.

Whares were **sacred** buildings where the Maori believed they were in the presence of their ancestors. These buildings were decorated with intricate carvings and weaving. Some sub-tribes also built whares, where they could gather with their own family and call upon their ancestors.

Each tribe had a chief, or *rangatira*. The chief had a **privileged** life. He lived, dressed, and ate very well. Some chiefs had more than one wife. Chiefs could also have **slaves**. These slaves were usually people who were captured during wars. Each village had a *tohunga*, who was a healer, wise man, or priest.

A whare is an important place for the Maori community to gather for meetings, rituals, and other cultural events.

Some tribe members belonged to a higher **rank**. Others belonged to a lower rank. Rank was not based on a person's possessions. Instead, rank was often determined by how much work a person did for the tribe. People who served or provided the most for the village had the highest ranks. Rank was also determined by family status. Being a chief's close relative gave a person a higher standing in the village.

Warfare was a part of Maori life. Preparing for battle was also a social **rite** of passage. Boys were expected to be warriors. At a young age, they learned **martial arts** and how to use weapons. Weapons were made from wood, whalebone, and greenstone, which is a type of very hard stone called jade. Preserving the tribe's honor was often a reason to go to war. Prestige, or *mana*, was extremely important to the Maori. Warriors wanted to protect their own mana and try to damage the mana of the other tribes.

Maori men performed a dance called the *haka* to prepare for battle. This dance included heavy stomping, loud chanting, and aggressive body movements.

THE SEASONS

New Zealand's seasons are opposite to the Northern Hemisphere. December through February is summer. These are the warmest months. March through May is autumn. June through August is winter. Spring is September through November. November is the rainiest month.

Communication

Public speaking was an important form of communication for the Maori. Any person who could inspire through speaking was held in high regard. The Maori did not have a written language until missionaries arrived in the 1800s. As a result, the spoken word became very important and valued. Public speaking included giving speeches, reciting poetry, singing songs, chanting, passing on history, or telling a joke or a story. It was a form of expression.

Stories were passed down orally from one **generation** to the next. Gifted storytellers spoke poetically. They would repeat stories and legends in

Songs, called *waiata*, help to preserve Maori knowledge and culture. There are many kinds of waiata. They may deal with themes such as love, loss, or even a child's lullaby.

The Changing Language

Originally, the Maori language was a **dialect** of Polynesian. Eventually, the Maori language developed its own characteristics. Over time, the Maori language changed to include words that describe European items or events.

For example, the Maori borrowed the word *ho-iho* from the English word "horse," and the word *ta-one* from the English word "*town*."

great detail. The storyteller's voice became soft, loud, or angry to make a story more dramatic and to show many emotions. Songs were often sung within the telling of a story. The storyteller would also move about and make arm gestures, jump, or walk to add to the story.

Songs told stories, as well. Songs expressed what was important to the Maori by using words about nature, traditions, or even jokes. Many of the songs the Maori sing today are about mourning or love. Maori women composed many of these love songs.

The *hongi* is a traditional Maori greeting. It is similar to a handshake. Two people press their noses and foreheads lightly together to exchange the *ha*, or breath of life.

Before missionaries created a written language, the Maori used a series of carving signs and knots to communicate. European missionaries used the English alphabet to represent the different sounds they heard in the Maori language. Only 15 letters or letter combinations are used to write the sounds of Maori words. These letters and combinations are h, k, m, n, p, r, t, w, a, e, i, o, u, wh, and ng. Each syllable ends with a vowel sound.

The first Maori language dictionary was written in 1844. Bishop Henry W. Williams compiled the information for this dictionary. He believed that by learning about the Maori language and culture, he could convert more Maori to Christianity. Once the Maori learned to communicate by reading and writing, they considered these skills quite valuable.

The Maori have borrowed words from languages other than English, as well. For example, the Maori word *mi-ere* came from the French word *miel*, which means "honey."

Law and Order

Traditional Maori society did not need laws and government. Instead, the Maori lived their lives according to their sense of honor, or *mana*, and according to *tapu*. Tapu is similar in meaning to the English language word "taboo," which means something sacred or forbidden. Tapu governed their lives and their beliefs.

Many things in Maori society were considered tapu. These things were governed by the village's *tohunga*, or spiritual leader. Certain places, such as a marae, were tapu. Some objects were also tapu, as were certain activities and even people. People in a village were ranked, and it was tapu for members of a higher rank to touch objects that belonged to a person of a lower rank. Should a higher ranked person touch one of these objects, it was considered pollution. The reverse was much worse. If a person of a lower rank touched an object belonging to someone of a higher rank, the person of the lower rank could be sentenced to death.

Mount Ruapehu on North Island has a special importance in Maori mythology. Mountains have a tapu. This comes from the mana of Papatuanuku, or Mother Earth, who gave birth to all things.

Many items belonging to a chief were tapu. For example, a chief's house was tapu. Women could not enter his house unless a special ceremony was performed.

Food was often tapu, too. Some foods could not be eaten inside a home, especially a chief's home. Food cooked for a chief was tapu and could not be eaten by anyone of a lower rank. Even if the chief did not eat it, it was tapu for a person of a lower rank to eat the food.

It was rare for a member of the Maori community to act against the tapu. While breaking these tapu did not go unpunished, the Maori believed the real punishment would come from the gods. They believed terrible things would happen to someone who acted against a tapu.

Maori beliefs give order to their society. The Maori believe that the spirits of their dead climb down the roots of a Pohutukawa tree to reach the underworld.

In traditional Maori culture, a new home possessed a tapu. Women were not permitted to enter a carved house while it was being built, since this would hurt the mana of the tribe. After the house was built, a ceremony was required to take away the tapu so a family could live in it.

Celebrating Culture

Traditional Maori culture was centered around daily life and chores. Hunting, fishing, and growing crops were as much a part of Maori culture as they were a way to survive. Since most members of a Maori village were somehow related, all tribe members were responsible for and to each other.

Mothers and fathers raised their sons and daughters, but grandparents, aunts, uncles, and cousins sometimes watched or taught the children.

Elders used stories to teach children. The Maori have a rich oral history, and stories are passed down from one generation to the next. Chiefs were especially talented at public speaking. When a chief or any other tribe member told a story, this person tried to make it dramatic and entertaining to watch.

An important celebration is the Maori new year, called *matariki*. It is celebrated in the spring. The theme of matariki is the Maori connection to the land. During matariki, families spend time together, share stories, enjoy feasts, and sing and dance.

Dances, or *haka*, were performed as a way of showing happiness or in preparation for war. There were two types of haka before a war. One was performed without weapons. It was used to express the warriors' feelings. The other haka was called *peruperu*. It was usually performed before setting off into battle. The warriors would make fierce facial expressions, shout and grunt, stick out their tongue, and wave their weapons. This haka was used to invoke the god of war and warn the enemy of the fate that would soon come to them. These dances were performed in complete unity. A tribal elder inspected the warriors as the haka was performed. It was considered a bad omen if the group did not perform as one.

Fishing was an important part of Maori culture. Fish were believed to be the offspring of Tangaroa, the sea god. While fishing, the Maori followed certain rituals to avoid the anger of Tangaroa.

Although haka are no longer performed to prepare for war, many Maori groups still perform these dances. They do this to stay connected to their culture and their tribe. Tourists also enjoy seeing the lively performances at Maori theaters and festivals.

Today, the haka has become very popular partly due to its performance before New Zealand rugby team matches. Each year, many haka groups compete for a national haka championship in a festival called *Te Matatini*.

Haka are often passed from generation to generation. Modern haka can even include political themes.

The haka is popular in New Zealand. Some sports teams have their own haka that they perform before each game. The New Zealand Army has a haka that each recruit must learn and perform.

Art and Culture

Art is an important part of Maori culture. The Maori decorate the walls, pillars, and ceilings of their homes. They decorate their clothes, weapons, boats, personal objects, and their bodies.

Carving is an important form of art. History is passed on through storytelling, but it is also done through carvings.

When the Maori first settled in Aotearoa, their carvings were similar to that of other Polynesian groups. As they became a unique culture, they developed their own carving style from the materials available in their new surroundings.

Inside the traditional homes of Maori chiefs, the wood is carved with very detailed patterns. The Maori sometimes carve their ancestors' faces or their own face into the wood. The Maori also recreate the shapes of fish, whales, animals, or their gods.

A double or single spiral pattern called *pitau* is used on every Maori carving.

Maori war canoes, or *waka*, were up to 100 feet (30 meters) long and covered with fine carvings.

The Maori take great care when creating their carvings. The wooden handles of spears, knives, and other weapons also include detailed carvings. The stone that is used to make the point of a spear is created with just as much care as the carved handle. Carvings are also done according to tapu, which makes them even more meaningful.

Wood, especially from the totara and kauri pine trees, is a popular material to carve. Maori men also make carvings from whale's teeth, stone, bone, and seal ivory. Not every Maori man is a carver. It is a talent only honed by some, and these men have a high standing in the village. Master carvers teach children how to carve.

While men carve, women weave. Weaving takes just as much care as carving. Women use reeds or products from their crops, such as **flax**, to create their weaves. They make clothing, baskets, footwear, and panels that cover the walls of their homes. Women weave beautiful panes with various designs that **adorn** the walls between carved wooden pillars.

Maori women perform a traditional dance with balls attached to flax strings at their waist. The balls are covered with woven flax. Their skirts are also made from flax.

Maori Performance

Music and dance are important parts of Maori culture. Traditionally, the word *haka* is used to describe all kinds of performances, including dance. Often, warriors performed the haka before a battle. During this type of haka, warriors chanted loudly while stamping their feet and moving their arms. Each tribe has its own haka.

Festivals featuring these activities take place throughout the year. Many of the best Maori performers compete during these festivals. High school students participate in haka competitions as a way of learning more about Maori culture.

Dressing Up

Maori traditional dress is worn for ceremonies and cultural performances. Some clothing is made in the traditional way. Other clothing is made using new techniques and materials.

Maori women include detailed weaving on the clothes they make. Flax is the most common material used to make clothes. Women also make traditional clothes from cabbage-tree leaves, dog skin and fur, feathers, and sometimes even human hair. Traditional garments are often stiff and uncomfortable. All the materials are woven together by hand. The women do not use **looms**.

Historically, girls were taught how to weave at a very young age. It was a skill all girls needed to learn. The tohunga blessed especially talented weavers.

Maori men and women wore different styles of clothing, as did people of higher or lower ranks. The Maori also wore different clothing for special occasions. While garments made out of dog skin were at one time the most prized clothing items, those made out of feathers from the kiwi bird became more prestigious over time. The Maori adorned themselves with pendants, combs, and feathers as a way to decorate their clothing.

Maori enjoy weaving traditional *putiputi* flowers from *harakete*, or flax. They wear the flowers on their clothing as a decoration.

Another way the Maori decorate themselves is by tattooing their skin. Tattooing was traditionally considered a way to carve the skin. The Maori cut patterns into their skin using tiny **chisels**. Then, they would tap dye into the cuts. It was a long and painful process. However, tattoos were considered to be full of mana. Most Maori men tattooed their bodies. They made designs on their faces, thighs, and buttocks. The head was considered the most sacred part of the body, so the head was very elaborately tattooed. If a Maori woman tattooed her face, it was usually along the upper lip, around the nostrils, or on the chin.

Tattooing different parts of the face was symbolic of many things. For example, a man's forehead was tattooed with his rank. Tattoos beneath a man's eyes were related to his family tree. Tattooing the part of the face that is directly in front of the ears showed if a man was married.

Traditional Maori tattooing was very painful. A person who was being tattooed could not eat solid food. Instead, liquid food was served through a wooden funnel.

Cloaks for Cover

Maori women practice special weaving methods to create traditional **cloaks**. These cloaks, which are made to honor a family member or a tribe member, take many months of preparing and hand weaving to create. Cloaks are often made from flax fiber.

Cloaks are often passed down from one generation to the next. These cloaks are highly valued, and the Maori wear them for special occasions, such as graduation and ceremonies. Today, only a few Maori women are able to make traditional cloaks.

Food and Fun

The Maori brought their most important crop with them from Polynesia. This crop was called *kumara*, and it was similar to a sweet potato. Kumara was a main staple in the Maori diet. At first, the Maori had difficulty growing kumara on Aotearoa, but they found ways to make this crop grow well in their new climate. They also found ways to store the kumara during the colder winter months.

Since all the members of a village hunted and grew food as a group, they also stored, cooked, and ate their food together. Kumara was stored in large, deep, cool pits that were built on hillsides. Proper food storage was very important. In fact, the Maori created storehouses, called *patakas*, for food.

The Maori cooked their food in a pit called a *hangi* or *umu*. Food cooked in this way is very tender, with a unique, earthy flavor.

Like all buildings, patakas were decorated with carvings. These carvings were **fertility** symbols, which the Maori hoped would encourage the gods to provide a generous supply of food.

Maori Diet

Tui

Watercress

Crayfish

Eels

The Maori traditionally ate a varied diet of animal and plant foods.

Crabs

Salmon

Kumara

Shellfish

Seals

Kereru

- Fruits and Vegetables
- Seafood
- Birds

The Maori were skilled hunters and fishers. They wove flax nets to catch fish. They carved fishhooks from bone and stone. The Maori also used spears to hunt birds and fish.

Birds, fish, seals, shellfish, and sometimes whales were other foods that were part of the Maori's diet. The Maori cooked food in an area that was not located near where they lived and slept. It was tapu to live and eat in the same building. Often, they cooked food out in the open air or in a shelter. Many families ate together. They cooked their food in a large pit called a *hangi* or *umu*. The Maori placed stones over an open fire. They placed a layer of green flax on top of the stones. Meat and vegetables were placed on top of the flax and then covered with another piece of flax. The Maori covered the oven with a mat. Then, they poured water over the stones to steam the food. Maori sometimes use these same cooking methods today.

Children and adults enjoyed playing games and having fun. They played many games that taught them valuable skills. For example, young boys threw soft spears at each other to practice their battle skills. Boys also enjoyed walking on stilts.

The Maori spent a great deal of time around the water. Young Maori would swing from ropes into a river or water below. They would also body surf in the ocean.

Kites were mostly flown by children, but the village tohunga had his own special version of a kite. String games, puppets, and playing musical instruments, such as a flute made from wood or a trumpet made from shells, were also forms of entertainment. Today, many Maori still enjoy themselves in much the same way.

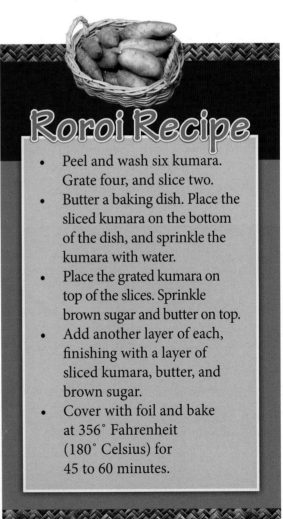

Roroi Recipe

- Peel and wash six kumara. Grate four, and slice two.
- Butter a baking dish. Place the sliced kumara on the bottom of the dish, and sprinkle the kumara with water.
- Place the grated kumara on top of the slices. Sprinkle brown sugar and butter on top.
- Add another layer of each, finishing with a layer of sliced kumara, butter, and brown sugar.
- Cover with foil and bake at 356° Fahrenheit (180° Celsius) for 45 to 60 minutes.

The Maori make musical instruments from wood. The *rehu* is a long flute that is played by blowing into a hole in its side.

Great Ideas

Traditionally, the Maori depended on items they found in nature for their survival. As a result, they respected all aspects of nature. This included trees, water, land, birds, and all animals.

As a form of respect, the Maori named large trees. When they needed to cut down one of these trees, the Maori held a ceremony to honor the tree. The tree was then used to build items such as shelters or weapons for hunting and battles. No matter how the tree was used, it was likely carved and decorated.

The Maori carve beautiful jewelry from greenstone. Greenstone, or jade, occurs naturally on South Island.

Although weapons or ornaments made from greenstone have been found on both the North Island and South Island of Aotearoa, the stone used to create these items came from the South Island. This meant that the Maori traded with or gave generous gifts to other villages. While many Maori tribes warred with each other, others also visited and benefited from each other. When one tribe visited another tribe, the visiting tribe brought gifts of thanks to their hosts. Later, the host tribe was invited to visit the tribe they had hosted. The original host tribe brought even more generous gifts to their new hosts. Tribes from the South Island may have given gifts of greenstone-tipped spears when they visited northern tribes. A coastal tribe may have given a generous portion of fish to a village that was inland.

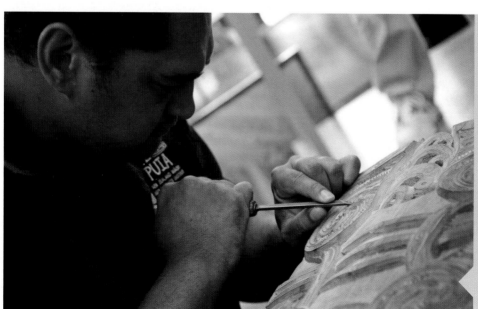

Wood is a very important part of Maori culture. Homes, boats, weapons, and spiritual artifacts are made from wood products. Maori carvings are famous for their elaborate detail.

While many Maori tribes had friendly relations, others sometimes fought in wars. The Maori had many war strategies. When the Maori began living in larger villages with more families, they built these villages in places that were safe from attack, such as on hills, along rivers, or by the sea. Much like a fort, great walls surrounded these villages. These villages were called *pa*.

Hand-to-hand combat was not the only way the Maori fought their wars. They prided themselves on tricking their enemy. Sometimes, a visiting tribe might attack their host tribe during a feast. Surprising the tribe that was under attack was often key to a victory. However, it was not uncommon for a tribe to feed their hungry opposers to ensure they were fighting on an "even" playing field. An easy victory over weaker opponents was not as honorable. Honor was very important to the Maori.

A war party followed certain rituals before battle, such as avoiding certain foods. Warriors performed a haka called *peruperu* before battle. This haka was dedicated to Tumatauenga, the god of war.

Weapons for War

The Maori had many special battle weapons. They carved weapons out of greenstone, wood, and bone. Each warrior had his own weapon, which was carved with a special symbol. The Maori used many weapons for war, but there were three main weapons. These weapons could kill even the strongest warrior with only one hit.

The *taiaha* was a long, pointed staff that looked like a spear. The pointed end was carved in the shape of a face that had paua shell eyes and a long, pointed tongue. The Maori used feathers and dog hair to decorate the shaft just below the face. *Patu* were short clubs that warriors wore on their flax belts. The Maori used this weapon to strike or beat their enemies. The *tewhatewha* had a long handle with an axe-like blade at one end and a point at the other end.

At Issue

The Maori worked hard to maintain their culture as Pakeha settlements increased and the Maori population declined.

When the Pakeha arrived on Aotearoa, it was not long before the land officially became New Zealand. This newly formed country was part of the British Empire. Although there had been battles between the Maori and the Pakeha, the Maori agreed to live under British rule. In 1840, the Maori and the British government signed the Treaty of Waitangi. This treaty was created to protect the Maori and the land they lived on, as well as to provide the Maori with the same rights as the British settlers.

Soon, Maori land was sold to Pakeha settlers, and the Maori were not allowed to live on some of the best land. From 1845 to 1870, more battles took place between the British and the Maori. The Maori were not successful.

By the 1870s, many Maori chiefs and their tribes had died in the land wars. In addition, the British government claimed more than 3 million acres (1.2 million hectares) of Maori land.

The Maori population was quickly declining. Many Maori were killed in the Maori Wars. Thousands of the Maori died from diseases that settlers brought with them from other countries.

When the British government took control of Aotearoa, money became important for survival. The Maori had not used currency in exchange for goods. This was a new idea for the Maori. Some Maori groups wanted to return to traditional ways and form their own societies. Other Maori tried to live the new life that was being introduced. With no money or means to live, more Maori died. By 1900, there were only about 40,000 Maori left. Many people referred to the Maori as a "dying race."

The Maori preserved their culture and traditional skills such as jade carving.

In order for the Maori to survive, they would need to fight. Due to the declining Maori population, battle was no longer an option. Instead, the Maori lobbied the government, negotiated deals, or hired lawyers to represent them in courtroom battles. Since the 1980s, many historical treaty disputes have been settled. Usually, the Maori receive a formal apology for the way they were treated by the settlers. They also receive money and land.

In 1975, the Waitangi Tribunal was created so Waitangi Treaty claims could be researched. While the tribunal does not settle claims and disputes, it makes recommendations to the government. These recommendations suggest ways the claim may be resolved or whether the claim should be addressed. Claims are settled through negotiation with the government. In 2008, the government of New Zealand agreed to pay reparations to a group of seven Maori tribes for land it confiscated in the 1800s. The government issued an official apology.

Maori Land Protests

During the 1970s, the Maori continued to struggle for the land rights they were promised in the Treaty of Waitangi. Land protests became a powerful way to lobby the government. There were many land marches and protests, which helped lead to the creation of the Maori Affairs Amendment Act in 1974, the parliamentary election of two Maori representatives in 1975, and the creation of the Waitangi Tribunal in 1975.

In 1970, one of the largest protest groups, Nga Tamatoa, formed to lobby for Maori cultural identity and acknowledgement of Maori issues. In 1975, Dame Whina Cooper led the Maori land rights march from the top of the North Island to the Parliament buildings in Wellington. Maori protesters from all over Aotearoa marched alongside Cooper. In 1978, Eva Rickard led four years of non-violent protest to reclaim Tanui land, which was used for defense purposes and later made into a golf course. Thousands of Maori protested outside parliament in Wellington, New Zealand, on May 5, 2004. They wanted to stop the government from nationalizing the New Zealand shoreline that traditionally belonged to the Maori.

Into the Future

By 1769, there were fewer than 85,000 Maori living on the islands of Aotearoa. They needed to find new ways to survive and to build a strong community. Beginning in 1867, four Maori representatives could be elected to the New Zealand government. At first, the Maori did not realize the importance of political power. By the 1900s, some Maori groups understood the need to have political representation. These groups began forming their own political parties, such as the Young Maori Party.

In 1995, the Queen of England, Elizabeth II, apologized to the Maori for how they were treated when the settlers first arrived and for the great loss the Maori people and their culture suffered.

Some Maori leaders decided to find ways to make Western values work within their traditional values. They saw the importance of education, proper **sanitation**, and building a strong economy. These leaders and other Maori groups realized the need to maintain their traditional society, as well as acquire the benefits of modern technology. There was renewed interest in traditional ways of life. This rebuilding of the Maori culture continues today.

The Maori language is the basis of Maori culture. However, since it is a minority language, many believe it is in danger of dying out. In the past, Maori language was discouraged in the schools. This attitude created a negative self-image among Maori youths. In 1987, the Maori Language Act created the Maori Language Commission to promote the language to all New Zealanders. Though it is a minority language, Maori is recognized as the indigenous language of New Zealand. It is spoken daily by about 130,000 people.

The Maori population is increasing faster than the European population. In 2011, more than 650,000 people of Maori descent were living in New Zealand. This is 16 times greater than it was 100 years earlier.

Members of the Maori Party staged protests to help establish Maori property rights to the shore and seabed off Maori lands.

Role-play Debate

When people debate a topic, two sides take a different viewpoint about one idea. Each side presents logical arguments to support its views. In a role-play debate, participants act out the roles of the key people or groups involved with the different viewpoints. Role-playing can build communication skills and help people understand how others may think and feel. Usually, each person or team is given a set amount of time to present its case. The participants take turns stating their arguments until the time set aside for the debate is up.

THE ISSUE

Maori language is the foundation of Maori culture. In the past, the use of Maori language was discouraged in New Zealand schools. Maori could not be spoken in the New Zealand courts. In 1987, the Maori Language Act changed this. Maori is now an official language of New Zealand. The government continues to encourage the use of the Maori language by all New Zealanders.

THE QUESTION

Should the New Zealand government promote the use of the Maori language to put it on an equal footing with English?

THE SIDES

 NO

Pakeha (non-Maori): Speaking the Maori language encourages the Maori people to think of themselves as separate. This discourages young Maori from becoming part of New Zealand business and society.

 YES

Maori: Maori-English bilingualism creates positive attitudes toward Maori culture. Just because Maori is a minority language, it should not be pushed into the background. The language will die if the government does not encourage its use.

Ready, Set, Go

Form two teams to debate the issue, and decide whether your team will play the role of the Maori or the role of the Pakeha. Each team should use this book and other research to develop solid arguments for its side and to understand how the issue affects each group. At the end of the role-play debate, discuss how you feel after hearing both points of view.

World Cultures Quiz!

1 What name do the Maori use for European settlers?

2 Who was Abel Tasman?

3 Why did more early Maori settle on North Island than South Island?

4 According to Maori legend, who discovered North Island?

5 What is the name for sacred buildings where Maori believe they are in the presence of their ancestors?

6 What is a *tohunga*?

7 Why did the Maori men perform the dance called *haka*?

8 Who wrote the first Maori language dictionary in 1844?

9 What did it mean to the Maori if a certain place was thought to be tapu?

10 How do Maori women use flax?

Key Words

adorn to add beauty or decorate something

ancestor a person from a past generation

Aotearoa the traditional Maori name for New Zealand

chisels metal tools with a sharp edge that are used to cut or shape something

cloaks loose pieces of clothing that fasten around the neck

colony people who leave their native land to settle in a new territory

cultures groups of people who share certain customs, values, traditions, and beliefs

dialect a form of a language spoken in a different region

extinction: no longer living on Earth

fertility producing something, especially a great deal of it

flax a fiber made from a commonly farmed plant that has pale blue flowers

generation people of the same age living in a society or family

indigenous peoples the first settlers to live in a particular country or region

looms machines used to weave yarn or thread into cloth by weaving many strands together

martial arts fighting methods that use very specific movements

missionaries people who teach their religion to other cultures

moa a large ostrich-like bird that lived on Aotearoa; it could not fly and is now extinct

prestige a level of importance in the eyes of other people

privileged a person who has rights or benefits that not every person has

rank a position in society

rite a ceremonial act

sacred spiritual, religious, and holy

sanitation the use of special measures to ensure a clean environment; the proper disposal of sewage

slaves people who are forced to do physical work for other people

Index

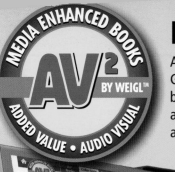

Log on to www.av2books.com

AV² by Weigl brings you media enhanced books that support active learning. Go to www.av2books.com, and enter the special code found on page 2 of this book. You will gain access to enriched and enhanced content that supplements and complements this book. Content includes video, audio, weblinks, quizzes, a slide show, and activities.

Audio
Listen to sections of the book read aloud.

Video
Watch informative video clips.

Embedded Weblinks
Gain additional information for research.

Try This!
Complete activities and hands-on experiments.

WHAT'S ONLINE?

Try This!	Embedded Weblinks	Video	EXTRA FEATURES
Map the area in which the Maori live.	Learn more about the Maori.	Watch a video of the Maori dancing.	**Audio** Listen to sections of the book read aloud.
Write a biography about a well-known person from the Maori.	Read about the history of the Maori.	See how the Maori live today.	
Create a timeline showing the history of the Maori.	View the arts and crafts of the Maori.		**Key Words** Study vocabulary, and complete a matching word activity.
Draw a chart to show the foods the Maori eat.			**Slide Show** View images and caption and prepare a presentatic
Test your knowledge of the Maori.			**Quizzes** Test your knowledge.

AV² was built to bridge the gap between print and digital. We encourage you to tell us what you like and what you want to see in the future.

Sign up to be an AV² Ambassador at www.av2books.com/ambassador.